D0577608

CREATIVE EDUCATION

MIAMI DOLPHINS

JULIE NELSON

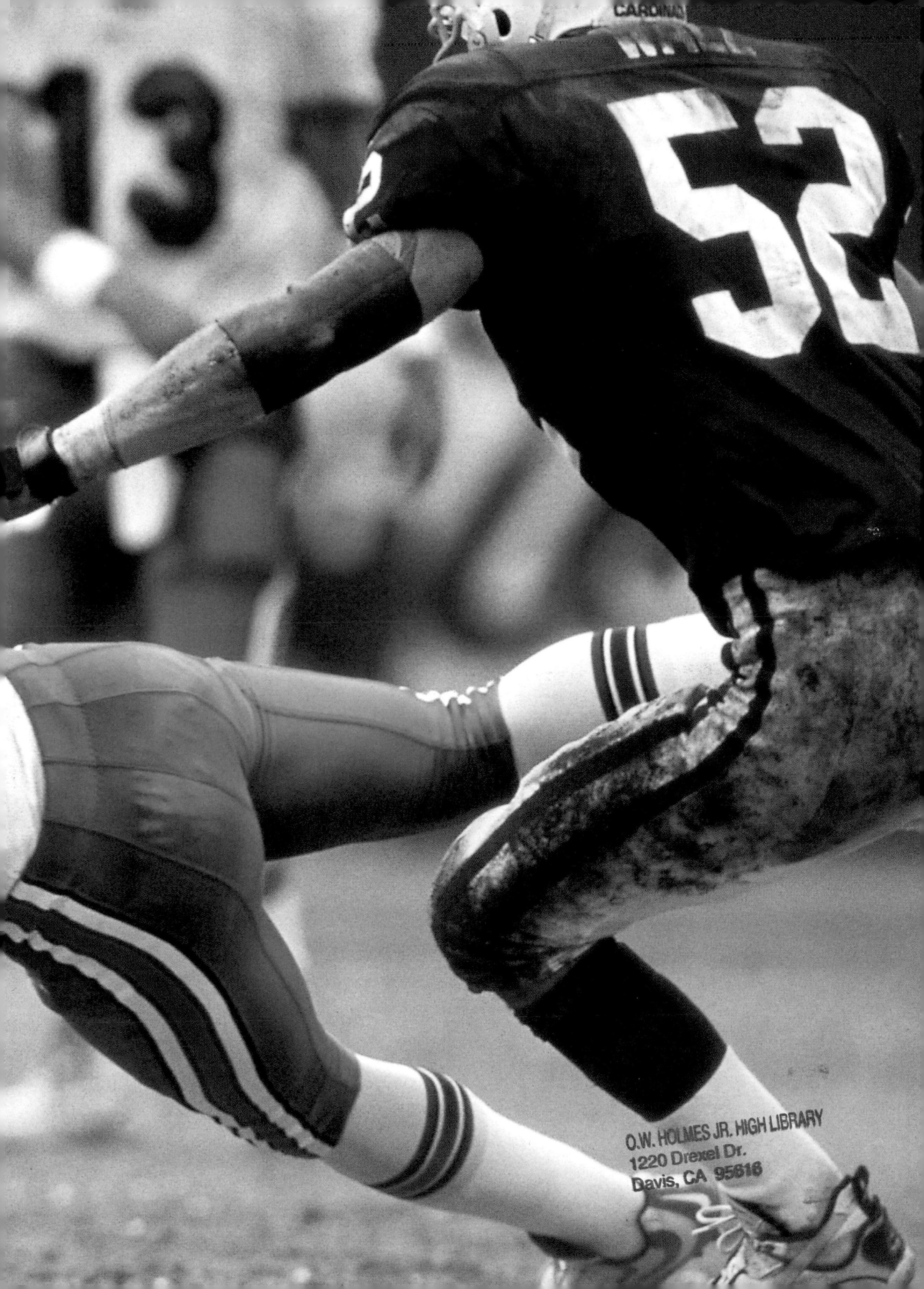

Published by Creative Education
123 South Broad Street, Mankato, Minnesota 56001
Creative Education is an imprint of The Creative Company

Designed by Rita Marshall

Photos by: Allsport USA, AP/Wide World Photos, SportsChrome

Library of Congress Cataloging-in-Publication Data

Nelson, Julie.
Miami Dolphins / by Julie Nelson.
p. cm. — (NFL today)
Summary: Traces the history of the team from its beginnings through 1999.
ISBN 1-58341-048-1

1. Miami Dolphins (Football team)—History—Juvenile literature. [1. Miami
Dolphins (Football team)—History. 2. Football—History.] I. Title. II. Series:
NFL today (Mankato, Minn.)

GV956.M47N45   2000
796.332'64'09759381—dc21   99-015758

First edition

9 8 7 6 5 4 3 2 1

With a year-round average temperature of 75 degrees and some of the best beaches in the world, it's no wonder Miami is one of the most popular vacation destinations in America. Built on the sun-drenched southeast coast of Florida, Miami is an oceanside hot spot that draws more than 10 million tourists a year.

Founded in 1870 by a Yankee settler named Julia Tuttle, Miami's population boomed in the 1920s as Americans discovered its sunny charms and flocked to buy houses there. In the 1960s, many Cubans immigrated to Miami, giving the city a large Spanish-American population.

Quarterback Dan Marino.

Bob Griese began his Hall of Fame career by throwing 15 touchdown passes as a rookie.

In addition to its great weather, Miami also boasts a number of successful sports franchises, including the Heat of the National Basketball Association and Major League Baseball's Marlins, the 1997 world champions. But Miami fans are perhaps most proud of their National Football League team, the Miami Dolphins.

For more than three decades, the mighty Dolphins have been a perennial powerhouse in the American Football Conference. During those years, they have won two Super Bowls and been represented by some of the greatest names in the history of pro football.

BUILDING A DREAM TEAM

Joe Robbie had a dream. The 50-year-old Minnesota lawyer was not a particularly rich man, but he wanted to own a football team, and he wanted to own one in Miami. So Robbie set out to persuade officials in the upstart American Football League to give him a franchise in Florida. In 1965, after months of talks, Robbie got what he wanted.

Robbie then held a contest, asking fans to suggest a name for the team. The most popular suggestion was the Dolphins. Robbie liked the name, pointing out that the dolphin is one of the fastest and smartest creatures of the sea.

The team didn't live up to its name at first. The 1966 Dolphins lineup included more than its share of over-the-hill veterans and finished last in its division with a 3–11 record.

In 1967, though, the team began its turnaround. That year, the Dolphins drafted a talented rookie quarterback from Purdue named Bob Griese. Griese, who wore glasses and was

Aggressive linebacker Zach Thomas.

Rookie fullback Larry Csonka ran through defenders for 540 yards.

known as "the thinking man's quarterback," had a strong arm and great poise under pressure. Over the next few seasons, coach George Wilson built up the team, signing running backs Larry Csonka and Jim Kiick and trading for halfback Mercury Morris, linebacker Nick Buoniconti, defensive end Manny Fernandez, and guard Larry Little, among other talented players.

Csonka, whose nickname was "Zonk," embodied a toughness that became a Dolphins trademark. Csonka decided he wanted to be a football player when he was nine years old, watching his older brother play high school ball. "Standing down around the bench, I took it all in—the coach and the players, the uniforms, the crowd, the lights," Csonka recalled. "It was a fantasy. And to be one of the players, that had to be the best part."

Csonka's high school coaches said he was too big to run with the ball. But Csonka proved them wrong and became one of the largest fullbacks to play the game. He attended Syracuse University before he was drafted by the Dolphins in the first round of the 1968 NFL draft. Csonka's running style was characterized by bulldozer-like strength and relentlessness. Csonka ultimately would become the Dolphins' all-time leading rusher with 6,737 yards on 1,506 carries. A five-time All-Pro player, he would be elected to the Pro Football Hall of Fame in 1987.

With Csonka's help, the Dolphins slowly improved. But by 1969, the team had yet to finish with a winning record, and its fans were getting restless.

Joe Robbie decided it was time for a change—and a new coach. He lured coach Don Shula away from the Baltimore Colts in 1970, but he had to give up Miami's first pick in the 1971 draft in exchange.

Robbie got a bargain. Shula would go on to appear in six Super Bowls, more than any other NFL coach. He also became the youngest coach to win 100 games, 200 games, and 300 games, and is the winningest coach in the history of professional football.

In 1969, the year before Shula arrived, the Dolphins sat at the bottom of the Eastern Division with a dismal 3–10–1 record. Shula knew he had his work cut out for him. "I am not a miracle worker," he said. "I have no magic formulas. The only way I know how to win is hard work."

The hard work paid off. Shula's debut 1970 season ended with a 10–4 record and included a six-game winning streak to finish off the year. Shula's luck, however, didn't hold in the playoffs, as the Dolphins lost a close one to the Oakland Raiders, 21–14.

The next year, the Dolphins went a step further, going 10–3–1, winning the AFC Eastern Division, and taking on the Kansas City Chiefs in the first round of the playoffs. With the score tied 24–24 with just 35 seconds left in regulation, Chiefs kicker Jan Stenerud lined up to try a 32-yard, game-winning field goal. The Kansas City crowd was confident. There was no way that Stenerud, an All-Pro, would miss.

The impossible happened. Stenerud missed and the game went into sudden-death overtime. Stenerud tried another

1 9 7 0

After kicking soccer balls in Europe, Garo Yepremian made the switch to American football.

9

Linebacker Nick Buoniconti led the Dolphins in tackles with 126 stops.

field goal, only to have it blocked by Miami's Nick Buoniconti and Lloyd Mumphord. The Dolphins' Garo Yepremian tried a 52-yarder, but it fell short. After the game went into a second overtime period, Larry Csonka made a 29-yard run to set up another field goal attempt. This time Yepremian drilled it, giving the Dolphins a 27–24 victory. By the end of the exhausting battle, the game had totaled more than 82 minutes—the longest game in pro football history.

Miami next trounced the Colts 21–0 in the AFC championship game to advance to Super Bowl VI to face the Dallas Cowboys. In the Super Bowl, the Cowboys' "Doomsday Defense" held the Dolphins offense to a single field goal, and Dallas won 24–3.

THE PERFECT SEASON

In 1969, Don Shula said, "My goals are the same every year—to win the Super Bowl, and we will do everything we can to do just that." Shula wanted every season to be perfect, and the 1972 season was—in more ways than one.

Even though Bob Griese broke his ankle in the fifth game of the season, the Dolphins offense remained unstoppable. Backup quarterback Earl Morrall led the AFC in passing, while Larry Csonka and Mercury Morris each rushed for more than 1,000 yards—a pro football first.

But the Dolphins defense also played a stellar role. Shula molded a group of largely unheralded players into the tightest defensive unit in the NFL. Nicknamed the "No Name Defense" because of their lack of famous names, the Dolphins allowed the fewest points of any NFL team in 1972. "The nickname doesn't bother us," said safety Jake Scott. "I don't care if people remember my name as long as we don't have any losses."

Scott's words proved prophetic. Miami finished 1972 with a perfect 14–0 record. It was the first time that any NFL team had gone undefeated since the Chicago Bears did so in 1942.

The winning streak continued in the postseason, as Miami edged out Cleveland and Pittsburgh in close AFC playoff battles. With a 16–0 record, Miami went into its second straight Super Bowl. Although the Dolphins were unbeaten, the NFC champs, the Washington Redskins, were still favored to win.

The Dolphins would not be thwarted in their quest for perfection. Jim Kiick scored the winning touchdown on a one-yard plunge, and Miami prevailed, 14–7. Don Shula had

1 9 7 2

Paul Warfield caught passes of 75 and 50 yards as Miami won the AFC title on January 2.

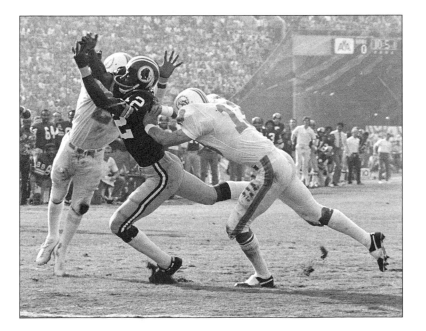

All-Pro safety Jake Scott (right) led the "No Name Defense."

Dominant pass rusher Jeff Cross.

to a 10–6 mark and an AFC Eastern Division championship. Sadly, Miami lost 34–19 to the Steelers in the playoffs, and Csonka, after 12 pro seasons, decided to call it quits.

In 1980, Griese, who had led the Dolphins for 14 years, was benched. It would be the final season for Griese, who had been a six-time All-Pro and put together a .698 winning percentage (91–39–1) under Coach Shula. A decade later, he would join Csonka in the Pro Football Hall of Fame.

In 1982, Miami was led by quarterback David Woodley, an eighth-round draft pick who had barely made the team. But under his leadership, the Dolphins posted a 7–2 record in the strike-shortened season and made it to the Super Bowl for the fourth time in franchise history. Then, Woodley's magic ran out. Led by their burly running back John Riggins, the Washington Redskins rolled over Miami 27–17 in Super Bowl XVII.

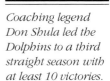

1 9 7 9

Coaching legend Don Shula led the Dolphins to a third straight season with at least 10 victories.

DAN THE MAN

The 1983 season was called "the Year of the Quarterback." There were several fine quarterbacks available in that year's NFL draft, including Dan Marino, who had starred at the University of Pittsburgh. Although Marino was selected in the first round by the Dolphins, he was still chosen behind four other quarterbacks. By midseason, Marino was the Dolphins' starting quarterback. In his first four starts, Marino led Miami to four wins and notched a 322-yard passing game against Buffalo.

With Marino on board, the Dolphins won nine of their last 11 games and captured the Eastern Division title in 1983.

Receiver Mark Clayton was a shifty runner (pages 18-19).

Marino, who led the AFC in passing, became the first rookie ever to start in the Pro Bowl.

The Dolphins played their first season in the brand-new Joe Robbie Stadium.

Miami fans had even more thrills in store in 1984. By the ninth game of the season, Marino had already broken Bob Griese's 16-year-old Dolphins record for most passing yards in a single season. Marino finished the year with league-leading totals in yards (5,084), completions (362), and touch-down passes (48). The yardage and touchdown marks are still NFL records.

Aided by the Miami defense—nicknamed "the Killer Bees" since nine players' names began with the letter "B"—the Dolphins surged to a 14–2 record, then pummeled Seattle and Pittsburgh in the playoffs. It was on to Super Bowl XIX, in which Marino predicted victory over San Francisco. Although Marino backed up his words with 318 passing yards on 29 completions, the 49ers won the game easily, 38–16, behind running back Roger Craig's three touchdowns.

In 1985, Marino guided the Dolphins back to the AFC championship game, which they lost 31–14 to the New England Patriots. Despite Marino's heroics, the Dolphins began to slide after that, failing to make the playoffs during the second half of the 1980s.

GETTING BACK ON TRACK

The Dolphins began the new decade on a brighter note. Their 12–4 record in 1990 earned them a trip to the playoffs, where they edged out Kansas City 17–16 before being eliminated by the Buffalo Bills, 44–34. The next year, despite 1,000-yard seasons from receivers Mark Duper and

Mark Clayton, Miami sagged. The Dolphins' defense had become weak; critics said that the famous No Name Defense had given way to simply no defense.

In 1992, the Dolphins won their division with an 11–5 record. They then crushed the San Diego Chargers 31–0 in the playoffs as Marino connected with tight end Keith Jackson for two touchdown passes. Two weeks later, however, the Super Bowl-bound Buffalo Bills eliminated Miami 29–10.

The Dolphins also started strong in 1993, winning three of their first four games behind the efforts of rookie running back Terry Kirby and receivers Mark Ingram and Irving Fryar. Then, in the fifth game of the season, disaster struck. Dan Marino tore his Achilles tendon and was sidelined for the rest of the season, and the team finished out of playoff contention.

1 9 9 3

Placekicker Pete Stoyanovich moved into second place on the Dolphins' all-time scoring list.

Keith Jackson was one of Dan Marino's favorite targets.

Outstanding safety Louis Oliver.

Any doubts that Marino could come back from his injury were dispelled in the 1994 season opener. More than 69,000 fans crowded into Joe Robbie Stadium to watch "Dan the Man" pass for 473 yards and five touchdowns in a 39–35 win over New England. "That's why he's Dan Marino," said Patriots coach Bill Parcells. "When you put up 35 points, you expect to win."

With Marino again leading the way, Miami emerged as a strong Super Bowl contender in 1994, finishing first in the AFC Eastern Division with a 10–6 record. In the playoffs, the Dolphins defeated Kansas City in the first round but fell 22–21 to the Chargers the next week.

Despite that disappointing loss, the season was a triumph for Coach Shula. At the end of the 1994 season, Don Shula's regular-season coaching record stood at 319–149–6, making him the winningest coach in pro football history.

1 9 9 5

Intense linebacker Bryan Cox led the Dolphins defense with 142 tackles.

GREAT MOMENTS AND MARINO'S MILESTONES

As the 1995 season began, Shula looked forward to building on his winning record with the help of a new crop of football talent in Miami, including running back Bernie Parmalee and tackle Tim Bowens, the 1994 Defensive Rookie of the Year.

Just as had been the case since 1983, though, the center of attention in 1995 was Dan Marino. Poised to take over the number one spot on the NFL's list of all-time quarterback leaders in four categories, Marino needed just 14 touchdown passes, 17 pass attempts, 1,830 yards, and 82 completions to top the career records set by the great Fran Tarkenton.

New coach Jimmy Johnson brought a disciplined approach and aggressive attitude to Miami.

It didn't take Marino long to make the records his own. After winning their first four games, the Dolphins faced the Colts. Marino needed just four completions to top Tarkenton's total of 3,686. He got 19, but Marino wasn't able to fully enjoy his achievement, as Miami blew a 24–3 halftime lead to lose 27–24.

"It was an embarrassment," said Don Shula after the game. "To see our unbeaten streak go down the drain in a game like this where we completely dominated in the first half is just an embarrassment to us."

The team continued to struggle, losing its next two games as well. But by the time Marino faced the Patriots in the ninth game of the season, he had another record in his sights. In the first quarter, he hit receiver Irving Fryar for a nine-yard gain, breaking Tarkenton's record of 47,003 career passing yards. Marino would rack up 47,299 yards by the day's end, but again the Dolphins lost, 34–17.

Two weeks later, in a rematch against the Colts, Marino threw a six-yard scoring pass to Keith Byars late in the second quarter. It was his 343rd touchdown pass—another record. More than 60,000 fans gave Marino a standing ovation, but the final result of the game was disappointing once more. Marino tossed three more scoring strikes, but it wasn't enough. The Dolphins lost 36–28.

After the game, Marino expressed his frustration. The record, he said, "is something I'm proud of. But we're not winning games. It's really hard to sit back and appreciate it."

By the end of the season, Marino had broken another of Tarkenton's all-time records: 6,467 pass attempts. He also finished second in the AFC in passing efficiency for the season. Miami finished 9–7 and earned a playoff berth, but they were destroyed 37–22 by the Buffalo Bills in their first post-season game.

Throughout the season, Coach Shula had come under increasing criticism. Miami radio stations blamed him for the Dolphins' failure to win the Super Bowl in the last two decades. In newspaper polls, the majority of Miami football fans said that Shula had to go.

On January 4, 1996, the 66-year-old coaching legend heeded the call and stepped down. "The time is right for me to resign," he said. Although Shula promised he would remain active in the organization, it was the end of an era. Coach Shula's record of 347–173–6 stands as one of the NFL's greatest achievements.

"The greatest coach in pro football is stepping aside," said Buffalo Bills coach Marv Levy. "All of us in coaching admire Don Shula as a person, and we revere his accomplishments. He sets an example for us all."

1 9 9 7

Linebacker Zach Thomas established himself as Miami's top tackler.

COACH JOHNSON TAKES THE REINS

Miami owner H. Wayne Huizenga soon announced that the Dolphins would hire Jimmy Johnson as head coach. Johnson had led the University of Miami Hurricanes to the national collegiate championship in 1987 and the Dallas Cowboys to two Super Bowl wins in the 1990s.

Johnson, only the third head coach in the team's history, made no bones about what he wanted from the Dolphins. "I expect results," he said tersely. "And as long as I get results, I'll be a very happy person."

Future Hall-of-Famer Dan Marino (pages 26-27).

1 9 9 8

Karim Abdul-Jabbar powered the Dolphins' ground game with 960 rushing yards.

Results in 1996 would be mixed. Fielding a roster of many of the youngest players in the NFL, the Dolphins finished the season 8–8. Among those young athletes was rookie halfback Karim Abdul-Jabbar. The speedy Abdul-Jabbar had played for three seasons at UCLA before entering the NFL draft. Taken by Miami as the 80th overall pick, Abdul-Jabbar soon proved to be a steal. In his first season with the Dolphins, he led the team with 307 carries for 1,116 yards and 11 touchdowns.

In 1997, the Dolphins went 9–7 behind Abdul-Jabbar's team-record 15 rushing touchdowns and another fine season from Marino. The Dolphins' final game of the 1997 regular season against the New England Patriots would determine the AFC East championship. Although Miami shut out the Patriots in the first half, New England managed to eke out a 14–12 victory. Six days later, the two teams faced off again, this time in the first round of the playoffs. Miami's offense managed only 162 total yards as New England again prevailed, 17–3.

Miami continued to improve under Johnson in 1998, finishing 10–6. The team's young, attacking defense—led by linebacker Zach Thomas, linemen Jason Taylor and Trace Armstrong, and cornerback Sam Madison—emerged as one of the finest in the NFL.

Offensively, Miami was led for the 16th season by Marino, who threw for another 3,497 yards. The 37-year-old quarterback's favorite target was speedy wide receiver O.J. Mc-Duffie, who racked up more than 1,000 yards for the first time in his NFL career. "He's a guy I rely on and can count on," Marino explained. "You can count on him to make big plays for you each and every week, no matter what the circumstances. He's a tough guy—he runs back kicks, he blocks downfield, and does everything you ask." Included in McDuffie's 1998 receptions was Marino's 400th touchdown pass, a new NFL milestone.

After beating the Buffalo Bills in the first round of the playoffs, the Dolphins went up against the defending Super Bowl champion Denver Broncos in what was to be the final matchup between two legendary quarterbacks. Marino and Denver quarterback John Elway were both members of the elite NFL class of 1983, yet this was only their third head-to-head meeting. Marino's Dolphins had triumphed in the first two matchups, including a 31–21 win on Monday Night Football only weeks before, a game in which Marino passed for 355 yards.

Unfortunately for Dolphins fans, Miami could not repeat the feat, falling 28–3. Denver went on to win the Super Bowl again, and Elway retired after the season, leaving Marino alone to push his many passing records further from the reach of up-and-coming NFL quarterbacks.

After the season, Marino announced his desire to continue playing for Miami. Although he had become the NFL's all-time passing leader in every major statistical category, Marino still lacked what he wanted most: a Super Bowl ring. "Just being a teammate of Dan Marino is something to cherish forever," said tight end Troy Drayton. "You see why he's going to the Hall of Fame. You know every time you catch the ball, it'll be a part of history."

Midway through the 1999 schedule, it looked as though the Dolphins were on their way to a historic season. A brash, hard-hitting defense carried the team to a 7–1 start in the tough AFC Eastern Division. In the second half of the season,

1 9 9 9

Speedy receiver Oronde Gadsden led the team with six touchdown catches.

Excellent blocker and clutch receiver O.J. McDuffie.

Star defensive end Jason Taylor.   31

2001

The Dolphins hoped that J.J. Johnson would emerge as a much-needed rushing threat.

however, Marino began to struggle with injuries. The quarterback's plummeting performance seemed to affect the entire team, as the Dolphins lost six of their last eight games and barely snuck into the playoffs with a 9–7 record.

The Dolphins regrouped enough for a 20–17 playoff victory at Seattle, but their season came to a jarring end the following week in Jacksonville. The Jaguars took advantage of seven Miami turnovers to hand the Dolphins a 62–7 thrashing— the worst loss in team history. "I've never experienced a game like this in my life," said Marino. "Even as a kid, I've never had a game like this."

Only days after the stinging defeat, Jimmy Johnson brought his Miami coaching career to an end. Hired in his place was Dave Wannstedt, who had coached the Chicago Bears before serving as Johnson's assistant in Miami. "We didn't win a championship, but we've got a lot of young talent," Johnson said. "There's no reason we can't move up from here."

Although Marino brought his career to a close after the season, Miami added to its offense by signing free agent quarterback Jay Fiedler and former Bills halfback Thurman Thomas. With Coach Wannstedt guiding this roster of talent, the Dolphins' future looks as bright as the Florida sun. The glory years of Dan Marino may be gone, but Miami fans are confident that greatness is just around the corner again.